I0790690

THE
WI-FI
PASSWORD

· · · · · · · · · · · · · · · · · · · ·

| Name: |
| Website Address: |
| ID/Username: |
| Password: |
| Notes: |

| Name: |
| Website Address: |
| ID/Username: |
| Password: |
| Notes: |

| Name: |
| Website Address: |
| ID/Username: |
| Password: |
| Notes: |

| Name: |
| Website Address: |
| ID/Username: |
| Password: |
| Notes: |

Name:

Website Address:

ID/Username:

Password:

Notes:

Name:

Website Address:

ID/Username:

Password:

Notes:

Name:

Website Address:

ID/Username:

Password:

Notes:

Name:

Website Address:

ID/Username:

Password:

Notes:

| Name: |
| Website Address: |
| ID/Username: |
| Password: |
| Notes: |
| |
| |

| Name: |
| Website Address: |
| ID/Username: |
| Password: |
| Notes: |
| |
| |

| Name: |
| Website Address: |
| ID/Username: |
| Password: |
| Notes: |
| |
| |

| Name: |
| Website Address: |
| ID/Username: |
| Password: |
| Notes: |
| |
| |

| Name: |
| Website Address: |
| ID/Username: |
| Password: |
| Notes: |

| Name: |
| Website Address: |
| ID/Username: |
| Password: |
| Notes: |

| Name: |
| Website Address: |
| ID/Username: |
| Password: |
| Notes: |

| Name: |
| Website Address: |
| ID/Username: |
| Password: |
| Notes: |

Name:

Website Address:

ID/Username:

Password:

Notes:

Name:

Website Address:

ID/Username:

Password:

Notes:

Name:

Website Address:

ID/Username:

Password:

Notes:

Name:

Website Address:

ID/Username:

Password:

Notes:

| Name: |
| Website Address: |
| ID/Username: |
| Password: |
| Notes: |

| Name: |
| Website Address: |
| ID/Username: |
| Password: |
| Notes: |

| Name: |
| Website Address: |
| ID/Username: |
| Password: |
| Notes: |

| Name: |
| Website Address: |
| ID/Username: |
| Password: |
| Notes: |

Name:

Website Address:

ID/Username:

Password:

Notes:

Name:

Website Address:

ID/Username:

Password:

Notes:

Name:

Website Address:

ID/Username:

Password:

Notes:

Name:

Website Address:

ID/Username:

Password:

Notes:

Name:

Website Address:

ID/Username:

Password:

Notes:

Name:

Website Address:

ID/Username:

Password:

Notes:

Name:

Website Address:

ID/Username:

Password:

Notes:

Name:

Website Address:

ID/Username:

Password:

Notes:

Name:

Website Address:

ID/Username:

Password:

Notes:

Name:

Website Address:

ID/Username:

Password:

Notes:

Name:

Website Address:

ID/Username:

Password:

Notes:

Name:

Website Address:

ID/Username:

Password:

Notes:

Name:

Website Address:

ID/Username:

Password:

Notes:

Name:

Website Address:

ID/Username:

Password:

Notes:

Name:

Website Address:

ID/Username:

Password:

Notes:

Name:

Website Address:

ID/Username:

Password:

Notes:

| Name: |
| Website Address: |
| ID/Username: |
| Password: |
| Notes: |

| Name: |
| Website Address: |
| ID/Username: |
| Password: |
| Notes: |

| Name: |
| Website Address: |
| ID/Username: |
| Password: |
| Notes: |

| Name: |
| Website Address: |
| ID/Username: |
| Password: |
| Notes: |

Name:
Website Address:
ID/Username:
Password:
Notes:

Name:
Website Address:
ID/Username:
Password:
Notes:

Name:
Website Address:
ID/Username:
Password:
Notes:

Name:
Website Address:
ID/Username:
Password:
Notes:

Name:

Website Address:

ID/Username:

Password:

Notes:

Name:

Website Address:

ID/Username:

Password:

Notes:

Name:

Website Address:

ID/Username:

Password:

Notes:

Name:

Website Address:

ID/Username:

Password:

Notes:

Name:

Website Address:

ID/Username:

Password:

Notes:

Name:

Website Address:

ID/Username:

Password:

Notes:

Name:

Website Address:

ID/Username:

Password:

Notes:

Name:

Website Address:

ID/Username:

Password:

Notes:

| Name: |
| Website Address: |
| ID/Username: |
| Password: |
| Notes: |

| Name: |
| Website Address: |
| ID/Username: |
| Password: |
| Notes: |

| Name: |
| Website Address: |
| ID/Username: |
| Password: |
| Notes: |

| Name: |
| Website Address: |
| ID/Username: |
| Password: |
| Notes: |

Name:

Website Address:

ID/Username:

Password:

Notes:

Name:

Website Address:

ID/Username:

Password:

Notes:

Name:

Website Address:

ID/Username:

Password:

Notes:

Name:

Website Address:

ID/Username:

Password:

Notes:

Name:

Website Address:

ID/Username:

Password:

Notes:

Name:

Website Address:

ID/Username:

Password:

Notes:

Name:

Website Address:

ID/Username:

Password:

Notes:

Name:

Website Address:

ID/Username:

Password:

Notes:

Name:
Website Address:
ID/Username:
Password:
Notes:

Name:
Website Address:
ID/Username:
Password:
Notes:

Name:
Website Address:
ID/Username:
Password:
Notes:

Name:
Website Address:
ID/Username:
Password:
Notes:

Name:

Website Address:

ID/Username:

Password:

Notes:

Name:

Website Address:

ID/Username:

Password:

Notes:

Name:

Website Address:

ID/Username:

Password:

Notes:

Name:

Website Address:

ID/Username:

Password:

Notes:

Name:

Website Address:

ID/Username:

Password:

Notes:

Name:

Website Address:

ID/Username:

Password:

Notes:

Name:

Website Address:

ID/Username:

Password:

Notes:

Name:

Website Address:

ID/Username:

Password:

Notes:

Name:

Website Address:

ID/Username:

Password:

Notes:

Name:

Website Address:

ID/Username:

Password:

Notes:

Name:

Website Address:

ID/Username:

Password:

Notes:

Name:

Website Address:

ID/Username:

Password:

Notes:

Name:

Website Address:

ID/Username:

Password:

Notes:

Name:

Website Address:

ID/Username:

Password:

Notes:

Name:

Website Address:

ID/Username:

Password:

Notes:

Name:

Website Address:

ID/Username:

Password:

Notes:

| Name: |
| Website Address: |
| ID/Username: |
| Password: |
| Notes: |

| Name: |
| Website Address: |
| ID/Username: |
| Password: |
| Notes: |

| Name: |
| Website Address: |
| ID/Username: |
| Password: |
| Notes: |

| Name: |
| Website Address: |
| ID/Username: |
| Password: |
| Notes: |

Name:
Website Address:
ID/Username:
Password:
Notes:

Name:
Website Address:
ID/Username:
Password:
Notes:

Name:
Website Address:
ID/Username:
Password:
Notes:

Name:
Website Address:
ID/Username:
Password:
Notes:

Name:

Website Address:

ID/Username:

Password:

Notes:

Name:

Website Address:

ID/Username:

Password:

Notes:

Name:

Website Address:

ID/Username:

Password:

Notes:

Name:

Website Address:

ID/Username:

Password:

Notes:

Name:

Website Address:

ID/Username:

Password:

Notes:

Name:

Website Address:

ID/Username:

Password:

Notes:

Name:

Website Address:

ID/Username:

Password:

Notes:

Name:

Website Address:

ID/Username:

Password:

Notes:

| Name: |
| Website Address: |
| ID/Username: |
| Password: |
| Notes: |

| Name: |
| Website Address: |
| ID/Username: |
| Password: |
| Notes: |

| Name: |
| Website Address: |
| ID/Username: |
| Password: |
| Notes: |

| Name: |
| Website Address: |
| ID/Username: |
| Password: |
| Notes: |

Name:

Website Address:

ID/Username:

Password:

Notes:

Name:

Website Address:

ID/Username:

Password:

Notes:

Name:

Website Address:

ID/Username:

Password:

Notes:

Name:

Website Address:

ID/Username:

Password:

Notes:

| Name: |
| Website Address: |
| ID/Username: |
| Password: |
| Notes: |

| Name: |
| Website Address: |
| ID/Username: |
| Password: |
| Notes: |

| Name: |
| Website Address: |
| ID/Username: |
| Password: |
| Notes: |

| Name: |
| Website Address: |
| ID/Username: |
| Password: |
| Notes: |

| Name: |
| Website Address: |
| ID/Username: |
| Password: |
| Notes: |

| Name: |
| Website Address: |
| ID/Username: |
| Password: |
| Notes: |

| Name: |
| Website Address: |
| ID/Username: |
| Password: |
| Notes: |

| Name: |
| Website Address: |
| ID/Username: |
| Password: |
| Notes: |

Name:

Website Address:

ID/Username:

Password:

Notes:

Name:

Website Address:

ID/Username:

Password:

Notes:

Name:

Website Address:

ID/Username:

Password:

Notes:

Name:

Website Address:

ID/Username:

Password:

Notes:

Name:

Website Address:

ID/Username:

Password:

Notes:

Name:

Website Address:

ID/Username:

Password:

Notes:

Name:

Website Address:

ID/Username:

Password:

Notes:

Name:

Website Address:

ID/Username:

Password:

Notes:

Name:
Website Address:
ID/Username:
Password:
Notes:

Name:
Website Address:
ID/Username:
Password:
Notes:

Name:
Website Address:
ID/Username:
Password:
Notes:

Name:
Website Address:
ID/Username:
Password:
Notes:

Name:

Website Address:

ID/Username:

Password:

Notes:

Name:

Website Address:

ID/Username:

Password:

Notes:

Name:

Website Address:

ID/Username:

Password:

Notes:

Name:

Website Address:

ID/Username:

Password:

Notes:

| Name: |
| Website Address: |
| ID/Username: |
| Password: |
| Notes: |

| Name: |
| Website Address: |
| ID/Username: |
| Password: |
| Notes: |

| Name: |
| Website Address: |
| ID/Username: |
| Password: |
| Notes: |

| Name: |
| Website Address: |
| ID/Username: |
| Password: |
| Notes: |

| Name: |
| Website Address: |
| ID/Username: |
| Password: |
| Notes: |

| Name: |
| Website Address: |
| ID/Username: |
| Password: |
| Notes: |

| Name: |
| Website Address: |
| ID/Username: |
| Password: |
| Notes: |

| Name: |
| Website Address: |
| ID/Username: |
| Password: |
| Notes: |

Name:
Website Address:
ID/Username:
Password:
Notes:

Name:
Website Address:
ID/Username:
Password:
Notes:

Name:
Website Address:
ID/Username:
Password:
Notes:

Name:
Website Address:
ID/Username:
Password:
Notes:

Name:

Website Address:

ID/Username:

Password:

Notes:

Name:

Website Address:

ID/Username:

Password:

Notes:

Name:

Website Address:

ID/Username:

Password:

Notes:

Name:

Website Address:

ID/Username:

Password:

Notes:

Name:

Website Address:

ID/Username:

Password:

Notes:

Name:

Website Address:

ID/Username:

Password:

Notes:

Name:

Website Address:

ID/Username:

Password:

Notes:

Name:

Website Address:

ID/Username:

Password:

Notes:

Name:
Website Address:
ID/Username:
Password:
Notes:

Name:
Website Address:
ID/Username:
Password:
Notes:

Name:
Website Address:
ID/Username:
Password:
Notes:

Name:
Website Address:
ID/Username:
Password:
Notes:

Name:

Website Address:

ID/Username:

Password:

Notes:

Name:

Website Address:

ID/Username:

Password:

Notes:

Name:

Website Address:

ID/Username:

Password:

Notes:

Name:

Website Address:

ID/Username:

Password:

Notes:

Name:

Website Address:

ID/Username:

Password:

Notes:

Name:

Website Address:

ID/Username:

Password:

Notes:

Name:

Website Address:

ID/Username:

Password:

Notes:

Name:

Website Address:

ID/Username:

Password:

Notes:

Name:

Website Address:

ID/Username:

Password:

Notes:

Name:

Website Address:

ID/Username:

Password:

Notes:

Name:

Website Address:

ID/Username:

Password:

Notes:

Name:

Website Address:

ID/Username:

Password:

Notes:

Name:

Website Address:

ID/Username:

Password:

Notes:

Name:

Website Address:

ID/Username:

Password:

Notes:

Name:

Website Address:

ID/Username:

Password:

Notes:

Name:

Website Address:

ID/Username:

Password:

Notes:

| Name: |
| Website Address: |
| ID/Username: |
| Password: |
| Notes: |

| Name: |
| Website Address: |
| ID/Username: |
| Password: |
| Notes: |

| Name: |
| Website Address: |
| ID/Username: |
| Password: |
| Notes: |

| Name: |
| Website Address: |
| ID/Username: |
| Password: |
| Notes: |

| Name: |
| Website Address: |
| ID/Username: |
| Password: |
| Notes: |
| |
| |

| Name: |
| Website Address: |
| ID/Username: |
| Password: |
| Notes: |
| |
| |

| Name: |
| Website Address: |
| ID/Username: |
| Password: |
| Notes: |
| |
| |

| Name: |
| Website Address: |
| ID/Username: |
| Password: |
| Notes: |
| |
| |

| Name: |
| Website Address: |
| ID/Username: |
| Password: |
| Notes: |

| Name: |
| Website Address: |
| ID/Username: |
| Password: |
| Notes: |

| Name: |
| Website Address: |
| ID/Username: |
| Password: |
| Notes: |

| Name: |
| Website Address: |
| ID/Username: |
| Password: |
| Notes: |

Name:

Website Address:

ID/Username:

Password:

Notes:

Name:

Website Address:

ID/Username:

Password:

Notes:

Name:

Website Address:

ID/Username:

Password:

Notes:

Name:

Website Address:

ID/Username:

Password:

Notes:

Name:

Website Address:

ID/Username:

Password:

Notes:

Name:

Website Address:

ID/Username:

Password:

Notes:

Name:

Website Address:

ID/Username:

Password:

Notes:

Name:

Website Address:

ID/Username:

Password:

Notes:

Name:

Website Address:

ID/Username:

Password:

Notes:

Name:

Website Address:

ID/Username:

Password:

Notes:

Name:

Website Address:

ID/Username:

Password:

Notes:

Name:

Website Address:

ID/Username:

Password:

Notes:

| Name: |
| Website Address: |
| ID/Username: |
| Password: |
| Notes: |

| Name: |
| Website Address: |
| ID/Username: |
| Password: |
| Notes: |

| Name: |
| Website Address: |
| ID/Username: |
| Password: |
| Notes: |

| Name: |
| Website Address: |
| ID/Username: |
| Password: |
| Notes: |

Name:

Website Address:

ID/Username:

Password:

Notes:

Name:

Website Address:

ID/Username:

Password:

Notes:

Name:

Website Address:

ID/Username:

Password:

Notes:

Name:

Website Address:

ID/Username:

Password:

Notes:

Name:
Website Address:
ID/Username:
Password:
Notes:

Name:
Website Address:
ID/Username:
Password:
Notes:

Name:
Website Address:
ID/Username:
Password:
Notes:

Name:
Website Address:
ID/Username:
Password:
Notes:

Name:

Website Address:

ID/Username:

Password:

Notes:

Name:

Website Address:

ID/Username:

Password:

Notes:

Name:

Website Address:

ID/Username:

Password:

Notes:

Name:

Website Address:

ID/Username:

Password:

Notes:

Name:

Website Address:

ID/Username:

Password:

Notes:

Name:

Website Address:

ID/Username:

Password:

Notes:

Name:

Website Address:

ID/Username:

Password:

Notes:

Name:

Website Address:

ID/Username:

Password:

Notes:

| Name: |
| Website Address: |
| ID/Username: |
| Password: |
| Notes: |

| Name: |
| Website Address: |
| ID/Username: |
| Password: |
| Notes: |

| Name: |
| Website Address: |
| ID/Username: |
| Password: |
| Notes: |

| Name: |
| Website Address: |
| ID/Username: |
| Password: |
| Notes: |

Name:

Website Address:

ID/Username:

Password:

Notes:

Name:

Website Address:

ID/Username:

Password:

Notes:

Name:

Website Address:

ID/Username:

Password:

Notes:

Name:

Website Address:

ID/Username:

Password:

Notes:

Name:

Website Address:

ID/Username:

Password:

Notes:

Name:

Website Address:

ID/Username:

Password:

Notes:

Name:

Website Address:

ID/Username:

Password:

Notes:

Name:

Website Address:

ID/Username:

Password:

Notes:

| Name: |
| Website Address: |
| ID/Username: |
| Password: |
| Notes: |

| Name: |
| Website Address: |
| ID/Username: |
| Password: |
| Notes: |

| Name: |
| Website Address: |
| ID/Username: |
| Password: |
| Notes: |

| Name: |
| Website Address: |
| ID/Username: |
| Password: |
| Notes: |

Name:
Website Address:
ID/Username:
Password:
Notes:

Name:
Website Address:
ID/Username:
Password:
Notes:

Name:
Website Address:
ID/Username:
Password:
Notes:

Name:
Website Address:
ID/Username:
Password:
Notes:

Name:
Website Address:
ID/Username:
Password:
Notes:

Name:
Website Address:
ID/Username:
Password:
Notes:

Name:
Website Address:
ID/Username:
Password:
Notes:

Name:
Website Address:
ID/Username:
Password:
Notes:

| Name: |
| Website Address: |
| ID/Username: |
| Password: |
| Notes: |

| Name: |
| Website Address: |
| ID/Username: |
| Password: |
| Notes: |

| Name: |
| Website Address: |
| ID/Username: |
| Password: |
| Notes: |

| Name: |
| Website Address: |
| ID/Username: |
| Password: |
| Notes: |

Name:
Website Address:
ID/Username:
Password:
Notes:

Name:
Website Address:
ID/Username:
Password:
Notes:

Name:
Website Address:
ID/Username:
Password:
Notes:

Name:
Website Address:
ID/Username:
Password:
Notes:

Name:

Website Address:

ID/Username:

Password:

Notes:

Name:

Website Address:

ID/Username:

Password:

Notes:

Name:

Website Address:

ID/Username:

Password:

Notes:

Name:

Website Address:

ID/Username:

Password:

Notes:

Name:

Website Address:

ID/Username:

Password:

Notes:

Name:

Website Address:

ID/Username:

Password:

Notes:

Name:

Website Address:

ID/Username:

Password:

Notes:

Name:

Website Address:

ID/Username:

Password:

Notes:

Name:

Website Address:

ID/Username:

Password:

Notes:

Name:

Website Address:

ID/Username:

Password:

Notes:

Name:

Website Address:

ID/Username:

Password:

Notes:

Name:

Website Address:

ID/Username:

Password:

Notes:

Name:

Website Address:

ID/Username:

Password:

Notes:

Name:

Website Address:

ID/Username:

Password:

Notes:

Name:

Website Address:

ID/Username:

Password:

Notes:

Name:

Website Address:

ID/Username:

Password:

Notes:

Name:

Website Address:

ID/Username:

Password:

Notes:

Name:

Website Address:

ID/Username:

Password:

Notes:

Name:

Website Address:

ID/Username:

Password:

Notes:

Name:

Website Address:

ID/Username:

Password:

Notes:

Name:

Website Address:

ID/Username:

Password:

Notes:

Name:

Website Address:

ID/Username:

Password:

Notes:

Name:

Website Address:

ID/Username:

Password:

Notes:

Name:

Website Address:

ID/Username:

Password:

Notes:

Name:

Website Address:

ID/Username:

Password:

Notes:

Name:

Website Address:

ID/Username:

Password:

Notes:

Name:

Website Address:

ID/Username:

Password:

Notes:

Name:

Website Address:

ID/Username:

Password:

Notes:

Name:

Website Address:

ID/Username:

Password:

Notes:

Name:

Website Address:

ID/Username:

Password:

Notes:

Name:

Website Address:

ID/Username:

Password:

Notes:

Name:

Website Address:

ID/Username:

Password:

Notes:

Name:
Website Address:
ID/Username:
Password:
Notes:

Name:
Website Address:
ID/Username:
Password:
Notes:

Name:
Website Address:
ID/Username:
Password:
Notes:

Name:
Website Address:
ID/Username:
Password:
Notes:

Name:
Website Address:
ID/Username:
Password:
Notes:

Name:
Website Address:
ID/Username:
Password:
Notes:

Name:
Website Address:
ID/Username:
Password:
Notes:

Name:
Website Address:
ID/Username:
Password:
Notes:

Name:

Website Address:

ID/Username:

Password:

Notes:

Name:

Website Address:

ID/Username:

Password:

Notes:

Name:

Website Address:

ID/Username:

Password:

Notes:

Name:

Website Address:

ID/Username:

Password:

Notes:

| Name: |
| Website Address: |
| ID/Username: |
| Password: |
| Notes: |

| Name: |
| Website Address: |
| ID/Username: |
| Password: |
| Notes: |

| Name: |
| Website Address: |
| ID/Username: |
| Password: |
| Notes: |

| Name: |
| Website Address: |
| ID/Username: |
| Password: |
| Notes: |

Name:

Website Address:

ID/Username:

Password:

Notes:

Name:

Website Address:

ID/Username:

Password:

Notes:

Name:

Website Address:

ID/Username:

Password:

Notes:

Name:

Website Address:

ID/Username:

Password:

Notes:

Name:

Website Address:

ID/Username:

Password:

Notes:

Name:

Website Address:

ID/Username:

Password:

Notes:

Name:

Website Address:

ID/Username:

Password:

Notes:

Name:

Website Address:

ID/Username:

Password:

Notes:

| Name: |
| Website Address: |
| ID/Username: |
| Password: |
| Notes: |

| Name: |
| Website Address: |
| ID/Username: |
| Password: |
| Notes: |

| Name: |
| Website Address: |
| ID/Username: |
| Password: |
| Notes: |

| Name: |
| Website Address: |
| ID/Username: |
| Password: |
| Notes: |

| Name: |
| Website Address: |
| ID/Username: |
| Password: |
| Notes: |

| Name: |
| Website Address: |
| ID/Username: |
| Password: |
| Notes: |

| Name: |
| Website Address: |
| ID/Username: |
| Password: |
| Notes: |

| Name: |
| Website Address: |
| ID/Username: |
| Password: |
| Notes: |

Name:
Website Address:
ID/Username:
Password:
Notes:

Name:
Website Address:
ID/Username:
Password:
Notes:

Name:
Website Address:
ID/Username:
Password:
Notes:

Name:
Website Address:
ID/Username:
Password:
Notes:

Name:

Website Address:

ID/Username:

Password:

Notes:

Name:

Website Address:

ID/Username:

Password:

Notes:

Name:

Website Address:

ID/Username:

Password:

Notes:

Name:

Website Address:

ID/Username:

Password:

Notes:

Name:

Website Address:

ID/Username:

Password:

Notes:

Name:

Website Address:

ID/Username:

Password:

Notes:

Name:

Website Address:

ID/Username:

Password:

Notes:

Name:

Website Address:

ID/Username:

Password:

Notes:

Name:
Website Address:
ID/Username:
Password:
Notes:

Name:
Website Address:
ID/Username:
Password:
Notes:

Name:
Website Address:
ID/Username:
Password:
Notes:

Name:
Website Address:
ID/Username:
Password:
Notes:

Name:

Website Address:

ID/Username:

Password:

Notes:

Name:

Website Address:

ID/Username:

Password:

Notes:

Name:

Website Address:

ID/Username:

Password:

Notes:

Name:

Website Address:

ID/Username:

Password:

Notes:

Name:

Website Address:

ID/Username:

Password:

Notes:

Name:

Website Address:

ID/Username:

Password:

Notes:

Name:

Website Address:

ID/Username:

Password:

Notes:

Name:

Website Address:

ID/Username:

Password:

Notes:

| Name: |
| Website Address: |
| ID/Username: |
| Password: |
| Notes: |

| Name: |
| Website Address: |
| ID/Username: |
| Password: |
| Notes: |

| Name: |
| Website Address: |
| ID/Username: |
| Password: |
| Notes: |

| Name: |
| Website Address: |
| ID/Username: |
| Password: |
| Notes: |

Name:
Website Address:
ID/Username:
Password:
Notes:

Name:
Website Address:
ID/Username:
Password:
Notes:

Name:
Website Address:
ID/Username:
Password:
Notes:

Name:
Website Address:
ID/Username:
Password:
Notes:

| Name: |
| Website Address: |
| ID/Username: |
| Password: |
| Notes: |

| Name: |
| Website Address: |
| ID/Username: |
| Password: |
| Notes: |

| Name: |
| Website Address: |
| ID/Username: |
| Password: |
| Notes: |

| Name: |
| Website Address: |
| ID/Username: |
| Password: |
| Notes: |

Name:

Website Address:

ID/Username:

Password:

Notes:

Name:

Website Address:

ID/Username:

Password:

Notes:

Name:

Website Address:

ID/Username:

Password:

Notes:

Name:

Website Address:

ID/Username:

Password:

Notes:

| Name: |
| Website Address: |
| ID/Username: |
| Password: |
| Notes: |

| Name: |
| Website Address: |
| ID/Username: |
| Password: |
| Notes: |

| Name: |
| Website Address: |
| ID/Username: |
| Password: |
| Notes: |

| Name: |
| Website Address: |
| ID/Username: |
| Password: |
| Notes: |

Name:

Website Address:

ID/Username:

Password:

Notes:

Name:

Website Address:

ID/Username:

Password:

Notes:

Name:

Website Address:

ID/Username:

Password:

Notes:

Name:

Website Address:

ID/Username:

Password:

Notes:

Name:

Website Address:

ID/Username:

Password:

Notes:

Name:

Website Address:

ID/Username:

Password:

Notes:

Name:

Website Address:

ID/Username:

Password:

Notes:

Name:

Website Address:

ID/Username:

Password:

Notes:

Name:

Website Address:

ID/Username:

Password:

Notes:

Name:

Website Address:

ID/Username:

Password:

Notes:

Name:

Website Address:

ID/Username:

Password:

Notes:

Name:

Website Address:

ID/Username:

Password:

Notes:

| Name: |
| Website Address: |
| ID/Username: |
| Password: |
| Notes: |

| Name: |
| Website Address: |
| ID/Username: |
| Password: |
| Notes: |

| Name: |
| Website Address: |
| ID/Username: |
| Password: |
| Notes: |

| Name: |
| Website Address: |
| ID/Username: |
| Password: |
| Notes: |

Name:

Website Address:

ID/Username:

Password:

Notes:

Name:

Website Address:

ID/Username:

Password:

Notes:

Name:

Website Address:

ID/Username:

Password:

Notes:

Name:

Website Address:

ID/Username:

Password:

Notes:

Name:

Website Address:

ID/Username:

Password:

Notes:

Name:

Website Address:

ID/Username:

Password:

Notes:

Name:

Website Address:

ID/Username:

Password:

Notes:

Name:

Website Address:

ID/Username:

Password:

Notes:

| Name: |
| Website Address: |
| ID/Username: |
| Password: |
| Notes: |

| Name: |
| Website Address: |
| ID/Username: |
| Password: |
| Notes: |

| Name: |
| Website Address: |
| ID/Username: |
| Password: |
| Notes: |

| Name: |
| Website Address: |
| ID/Username: |
| Password: |
| Notes: |

Name:
Website Address:
ID/Username:
Password:
Notes:

Name:
Website Address:
ID/Username:
Password:
Notes:

Name:
Website Address:
ID/Username:
Password:
Notes:

Name:
Website Address:
ID/Username:
Password:
Notes:

Name:

Website Address:

ID/Username:

Password:

Notes:

Name:

Website Address:

ID/Username:

Password:

Notes:

Name:

Website Address:

ID/Username:

Password:

Notes:

Name:

Website Address:

ID/Username:

Password:

Notes:

Name:
Website Address:
ID/Username:
Password:
Notes:

Name:
Website Address:
ID/Username:
Password:
Notes:

Name:
Website Address:
ID/Username:
Password:
Notes:

Name:
Website Address:
ID/Username:
Password:
Notes:

Name:

Website Address:

ID/Username:

Password:

Notes:

Name:

Website Address:

ID/Username:

Password:

Notes:

Name:

Website Address:

ID/Username:

Password:

Notes:

Name:

Website Address:

ID/Username:

Password:

Notes:

| Name: |
| Website Address: |
| ID/Username: |
| Password: |
| Notes: |
| |
| |

| Name: |
| Website Address: |
| ID/Username: |
| Password: |
| Notes: |
| |
| |

| Name: |
| Website Address: |
| ID/Username: |
| Password: |
| Notes: |
| |
| |

| Name: |
| Website Address: |
| ID/Username: |
| Password: |
| Notes: |
| |
| |

| Name: |
| Website Address: |
| ID/Username: |
| Password: |
| Notes: |

| Name: |
| Website Address: |
| ID/Username: |
| Password: |
| Notes: |

| Name: |
| Website Address: |
| ID/Username: |
| Password: |
| Notes: |

| Name: |
| Website Address: |
| ID/Username: |
| Password: |
| Notes: |

Name:

Website Address:

ID/Username:

Password:

Notes:

Name:

Website Address:

ID/Username:

Password:

Notes:

Name:

Website Address:

ID/Username:

Password:

Notes:

Name:

Website Address:

ID/Username:

Password:

Notes:

Name:

Website Address:

ID/Username:

Password:

Notes:

Name:

Website Address:

ID/Username:

Password:

Notes:

Name:

Website Address:

ID/Username:

Password:

Notes:

Name:

Website Address:

ID/Username:

Password:

Notes:

Name:

Website Address:

ID/Username:

Password:

Notes:

Name:

Website Address:

ID/Username:

Password:

Notes:

Name:

Website Address:

ID/Username:

Password:

Notes:

Name:

Website Address:

ID/Username:

Password:

Notes:

Name:
Website Address:
ID/Username:
Password:
Notes:

Name:
Website Address:
ID/Username:
Password:
Notes:

Name:
Website Address:
ID/Username:
Password:
Notes:

Name:
Website Address:
ID/Username:
Password:
Notes:

Name:

Website Address:

ID/Username:

Password:

Notes:

Name:

Website Address:

ID/Username:

Password:

Notes:

Name:

Website Address:

ID/Username:

Password:

Notes:

Name:

Website Address:

ID/Username:

Password:

Notes:

Name:

Website Address:

ID/Username:

Password:

Notes:

Name:

Website Address:

ID/Username:

Password:

Notes:

Name:

Website Address:

ID/Username:

Password:

Notes:

Name:

Website Address:

ID/Username:

Password:

Notes:

Name:

Website Address:

ID/Username:

Password:

Notes:

Name:

Website Address:

ID/Username:

Password:

Notes:

Name:

Website Address:

ID/Username:

Password:

Notes:

Name:

Website Address:

ID/Username:

Password:

Notes:

Name:

Website Address:

ID/Username:

Password:

Notes:

Name:

Website Address:

ID/Username:

Password:

Notes:

Name:

Website Address:

ID/Username:

Password:

Notes:

Name:

Website Address:

ID/Username:

Password:

Notes:

Name:

Website Address:

ID/Username:

Password:

Notes:

Name:

Website Address:

ID/Username:

Password:

Notes:

Name:

Website Address:

ID/Username:

Password:

Notes:

Name:

Website Address:

ID/Username:

Password:

Notes:

Name:

Website Address:

ID/Username:

Password:

Notes:

Name:

Website Address:

ID/Username:

Password:

Notes:

Name:

Website Address:

ID/Username:

Password:

Notes:

Name:

Website Address:

ID/Username:

Password:

Notes:

Name:

Website Address:

ID/Username:

Password:

Notes:

Name:

Website Address:

ID/Username:

Password:

Notes:

Name:

Website Address:

ID/Username:

Password:

Notes:

Name:

Website Address:

ID/Username:

Password:

Notes:

| Name: |
| Website Address: |
| ID/Username: |
| Password: |
| Notes: |
| |
| |

| Name: |
| Website Address: |
| ID/Username: |
| Password: |
| Notes: |
| |
| |

| Name: |
| Website Address: |
| ID/Username: |
| Password: |
| Notes: |
| |
| |

| Name: |
| Website Address: |
| ID/Username: |
| Password: |
| Notes: |
| |
| |

Name:

Website Address:

ID/Username:

Password:

Notes:

Name:

Website Address:

ID/Username:

Password:

Notes:

Name:

Website Address:

ID/Username:

Password:

Notes:

Name:

Website Address:

ID/Username:

Password:

Notes:

Name:

Website Address:

ID/Username:

Password:

Notes:

Name:

Website Address:

ID/Username:

Password:

Notes:

Name:

Website Address:

ID/Username:

Password:

Notes:

Name:

Website Address:

ID/Username:

Password:

Notes:

Name:

Website Address:

ID/Username:

Password:

Notes:

Name:

Website Address:

ID/Username:

Password:

Notes:

Name:

Website Address:

ID/Username:

Password:

Notes:

Name:

Website Address:

ID/Username:

Password:

Notes:

| Name: |
| Website Address: |
| ID/Username: |
| Password: |
| Notes: |

| Name: |
| Website Address: |
| ID/Username: |
| Password: |
| Notes: |

| Name: |
| Website Address: |
| ID/Username: |
| Password: |
| Notes: |

| Name: |
| Website Address: |
| ID/Username: |
| Password: |
| Notes: |

Name:

Website Address:

ID/Username:

Password:

Notes:

Name:

Website Address:

ID/Username:

Password:

Notes:

Name:

Website Address:

ID/Username:

Password:

Notes:

Name:

Website Address:

ID/Username:

Password:

Notes:

Name:

Website Address:

ID/Username:

Password:

Notes:

Name:

Website Address:

ID/Username:

Password:

Notes:

Name:

Website Address:

ID/Username:

Password:

Notes:

Name:

Website Address:

ID/Username:

Password:

Notes:

| Name: |
| Website Address: |
| ID/Username: |
| Password: |
| Notes: |

| Name: |
| Website Address: |
| ID/Username: |
| Password: |
| Notes: |

| Name: |
| Website Address: |
| ID/Username: |
| Password: |
| Notes: |

| Name: |
| Website Address: |
| ID/Username: |
| Password: |
| Notes: |

Name:

Website Address:

ID/Username:

Password:

Notes:

Name:

Website Address:

ID/Username:

Password:

Notes:

Name:

Website Address:

ID/Username:

Password:

Notes:

Name:

Website Address:

ID/Username:

Password:

Notes:

www.ingramcontent.com/pod-product-compliance
Lightning Source LLC
Chambersburg PA
CBHW031240250726
48655CB00005B/2031